Idle Mac's

Doggerel Bank

(Selected, compiled and edited by Colin Eston)

Idle Mac's

Doggerel Bank

Inconsequential Musings on Life by

Richard McIntyre Atkinson

1

~ Poet, Know thyself! ~

Sir, I admit your gen'ral rule
That every poet is a fool;
But you yourself may serve to show it,
That every fool is not a poet.

Alexander Pope

Thy drasty rhyming is nat worth a toord!

Geoffrey Chaucer

~ Poet, Know thyself! ~

Know Thyself

I am only a humble man,
Of little intellect and wit.
I write as I do, rather than
As those whose ideas lightly flit
'Midst things profound and serious
With shining power imperious.

Not 'M.' but 'McI.'

My middle name is McIntyre,
With all that may imply.
I am not one for wasting things,
Most certainly not 'I'.
My middle name is McIntyre,
A member of a clan.
Within my veins there runs the blood
Of a quarter Scotsman.
My middle name is McIntyre,
The name my father bore.
His mother carried the same name,
Her maiden name of yore.
My middle name is McIntyre
As is that of my son,
And so it is of his first child -
The name goes on and on.
I've said before that I waste not
And that indeed is true.
Why try to find another name
When McIntyre will do?

Parvum in Multo

So, I'm not good-looking
And no good at cooking.
However hard I try,
My pot plants always die.
And then, of course, what's more -
You know I cannot draw
And skilful's what I ain't
When I attempt to paint.
Then there's another thing -
I really cannot sing.
While everybody loathes
My personal taste in clothes.
My poor attempts at verse
Draw comments somewhat terse.
But let me at least claim
A modicum of fame:
At one thing I am great -
That's putting pictures straight!

Washing-Up

I stand and look while all around
The pots and pans and plates abound.
Soap and suds and an urge to swear,
My wife's asleep, she's done her share.
It's my turn now to get stuck in
Removing grease from baking tin,
Scraping mash from saucepan bottom,
Washing glasses till I've got 'em
Full of glint and pristine gleam
Row on row all sparkling clean.
Making sink and kitchen tidy,
Knowing that tomorrow – Friday -
Everyday the same old chore,
For, if we eat, there must be more!

Pro Arte

My wife's work is all around -
Art *chefs d'oeuvre* so abound
That there is no room now left
To place others, though she's deft
At re-hanging all she does
So there's space where once there was
No apparent place to site
Products of her fancy's flight.
In the bedroom, in the loo
(Where a lady stares at you)
In the hall and up the stair
There is not a place left where
She can squeeze another in
Howsoever small and thin.
As her output grows apace
I shall have to create space.
I'm afraid it really sounds
As if, somewhere in the grounds,
I shall be obliged to put
A prefabricated hut.
After that, it will behove
Us to up sticks and remove.

Bel Canto

A funny old thing is this singing.
You try for a note and go flat.
You turn to your wife who is wincing
And say, 'Now then! How bout that?'

'My God,' she replies with a shudder.
'It's worse than I normally hear
It sounds like a cow with sore udder -
You really must shut up, my dear!'

On receiving a 3D puzzle

(to the tune of My Bonny Lies over the Ocean)

Dear daughter, you bought a great puzzle
And kindly you sent it to me.
Dear daughter, you bought a great puzzle;
For God's sake please send me the key!
Send me, send me, for God's sake please send me the key, the key;
Send me, send me, for God's sake please send me the key!

Your mother has told me I've got it:
It's written in code on the sheet.
Your mother has told me I've got it.
I'm going upstairs now to cheat.
Upstairs, upstairs, I'm going upstairs now to cheat, to cheat.
Upstairs, upstairs, I'm going upstairs now to cheat!

I've looked in the mirror and got it.
What I've got to do now I see.
I've looked in the mirror and got it.
I'll have it all done before tea.
All done, all done, I'll have it all done before tea, 'fore tea;
All done, all done, I'll have it all done before tea!

I know what you're saying about me -
I hear it quite loud and quite plain.
I know what you're saying about me:
'I'll *never* buy *him* one again!
Never! Never! Never buy him one again, again.
Never! Never! Never buy him one again!'

Computer

*(written at my grand-daughter's request.
I later found that her teacher gave her 18/20 for it!)*

Computer in the room
Green
Screen
In the gloom.

Switch on
Log on
Go on and on
Along the byways
Of the information highway.

There is a mouse
In the house.
Let it scuttle round the screen
Green screen, green screen,
Let it scan from side to side
In the web that spreads worldwide.

Ranch Fencing

For more than a week I was down on my knees.
I do hope the results will finally please
All those passing by and who, seeing my work,
Did not simply regard me as some kind of berk.
While down on my knees, I've had all the remarks
(Though from dogs I've shooed off I've merely had barks)
Like 'Say one for me'; 'Get the shine right side out';
'Don't paint upside down', and from one who, no doubt,
Considered his words were exquisitely fine:
'When you've finished that, you can come and paint mine!'
When all's said and done, I've worked to the letter,
I've just tried to make my village look better.

Floreat Premium Bond

'Twas in the winter of Fifty-Seven
That Mum (Ah, God rest her!) now in Heaven,
Acting on principles ever so fond,
Bought, for my pleasure, a Premium Bond.
So that, ever since then from that day on,
I waited for prizes, but came there none.
Full forty-two years I waited in vain
With hopes dashed each month – no pain and no gain!
At last, in despair, I cashed the Bond in
And, clutching my pound, succumbed to black sin;
Thus, for the first time a scratch-card I bought,
Though from its purchase no profit I sought.
But, as I scratched, the silver grew thinner -
The symbols revealed made me a winner!
At last I have made it; I'm living in clover.
My Bond has repaid me a full nine times over!

Wintry Riding

When it is cold
Do not go out
A-riding on your bicycles.
For, if you do,
With a wet beard,
You'll end up clad in icicles.

The portent

'Draw nigh, good folk,' the old man said
High upon the hill.
The good folk came towards him, they gathered
And were still.
They stood there, all before him, in silence
And in awe,
A goodly host of people, five thousand souls
Or more.
'List well, good folk, and hear me, for I have
Much to say
And I shall tell it all,' said he, ' as night
Ends the day.'
So, faithfully, they stood there as hours slow
Passed by
Until, at last, 'mid shadows, the sun fled
From the sky.
And just as last light lingered, before the stars
Shone bright,
He gazed at those before him and looked from
Left to right.
Then, as the crowd stood silent, he oped his mouth
And said
'Forgive me! I've forgotten. I'm going home
To bed!'

2

~ Day to Day ~

Everything that happens happens as it should, and if you observe carefully, you will find this to be so.

Marcus Aurelius Antoninus

Life is just one damned thing after another.

Elbert Hubbard

~ Day to Day ~

The phantom bell-ringer of Back Lane

We thank you for your morning call
Though we do not need it;
We have a clock upon the wall
And we always heed it.
However, it is nice to know
You think of us each day
And that you'll call, come rain, come snow,
Each time you pass our way.
We're full of admiration for
Your timing – it's just great!
When the bell rings out at our front door
We know it's half-past eight.
But please, as you go 'cross our grass,
I hope that you will choose
A different way, each day, to pass
So finally we'll lose
The worm-casts that abound, around
Which with your feet you'll pat,
And we'll end up with level ground -
A tit for your (rat-) tat!

The Teapot

Gleaming greyly in the corner,
Hiding all its wounds away,
Silver plate upon base metal,
Losses shown by light of day -
Yet its state does not dismay me.
I recall where it came from:
Silver teapot of my mother -
Symbol of a hearth and home.

Souvenirs

Cast not aside those champagne caps.
They represent the passing lapse
Of time between events and acts
That marked our life and artefacts.

High Hopes

A while ago, as I recall,
A little *snap-thud* in the hall
Announced our normal morning mail
Arrival which can never fail
To bring a flutter to the heart
At the announcement of the start
Of a new day.

What can be in those envelopes?
Realisation of our hopes
Of a big win from Premium Bond?
Or news from those who correspond
By pen and paper and the post?
Or merely a flooding host
Of junk mail, say?

The Visitor

There's a little auburn beauty who visits every day
And his palest of pale green eyes look up and seem to say:
'Am I welcome in your house, sir? May I a short time stay?
I only need a little space, I won't get in your way.
And, please, I'd like a little milk, but only if I may,
And afterwards the lightest stroke beneath my chin, I pray.
Then, stretched upon your kitchen floor, my body I shall lay
And, having had my little rest, I'll gently steal away,
So the last you'll see of me is a curly tail a-splay.

On receiving a garden gnome

(It was well-known that plaster gnomes were objects I vociferously argued against and despised – yet my daughter still gave me one.)

Hello! My name is Agro Gnome.
When I'm not here, I'm not at home.
It's merely that I like to roam
Far from the land-locked fields of loam,
O'er the deep seas' whitening foam
Beneath the Earth's cerulean dome,
With hope of distant beach to comb.

The Dreadful Fate of Agro Gnome

(with thanks to McGonagall and the Goons)

'Twas in the year of ninety-three
Within the month of January
The wind did blow and it did moan
And brought the death of Agro Gnome.
Poor lad, a-standing in his lair,
With fix-ed smile in windy air,
The gusting gale he can't resist -
Oh! could it be that he was (*drunk*)?
He fell full length with shatt'ring crash
And gave himself an awful bash.
Spread in bits midst grass and clover,
Alas! That's Agro Gnome all over!
Oh! 'Twas not done deliberately;
He will live on in memory!

Limerick for Ibiza

It was fine till I stepped off the plane
And saw where I was to remain.
One look was enough.
I packed up my stuff
And flew back to my home once again.

Tempus Fugit

Oh where, oh where has my carriage clock gone?
Oh where, oh where can it be?
You promised I'd have it in twenty-eight days
And now it's at least thirty-three!
I've taken delivery of the Yorkshire Post
And read it with int'rest quite keen.
I read everything from the front to the back.
I even read B**!!?d Dineen!
I've fulfilled my promise for six months and more
Your canvassing callers confirm.
I've every intention of carrying on
(At least in the medium term.)
I use the term *medium* for I'm sixty-three
And unlikely to read it for ever,
For who knows what Fate has in store for me now?
She may my life-thread shortly sever!
How sad would it be if you dallied too long
And I never got my just due?
To have the tick-tock of my carriage-clock
Is totally now up to you!

Thoughts on Spanish customs

It's two a.m. and I'm in bed
But Spaniards now wake up instead.
A blast of brass, a stamp of feet,
And throbbing music fills the street.
Windows shake and glasses rattle.
I'm fighting a losing battle.
If it continues in this way
I'll need another holiday!

The Snowman uncovered

The snowman has finally lost his hat!
Now who would have thought it, who'd have thought that?
The brim is torn off, the body has gone,
The crown just lying there, looking forlorn.
How can a snowman exist with no hat?
It's just like a cat who hasn't a mat.
Like the Italian without his pet -
Romeo, that is, without Juliet.
Or all those others who would find it hard
Such as Heloise with no Abelard.
Think of our Mickey without his Minnie,
Just like a Geordie without his hinny.
One thing is certain, I am sure of that -
Respectable snowmen wear a top hat!
And that's that!

Eggsasperating yobbery.

Someone throws eggs in our garden
And onto our windows as well.
I know, for I see the presence
As lingering oviform shell.
It's not just the shell that's the trouble,
The contents are sticky and smell
For they cling to the panes of the double-
Glazing and set hard. Bloody Hell!
What pleasure it gives them eludes me -
Perhaps it's the unctuous squelch
That it makes as it slithers all slimy
Down the glass, like an over-rich belch!

3

~ *That's Life!* ~

*It's a funny old world –
a man's lucky if he gets out of it alive*

W.C. Fields

*If A is success in life, then A=x+y+z.
Work is x, y is play – and z is keeping your mouth shut.*

Albert Einstein

~ That's Life! ~

The laws of life

Children know better than adults.
All women know better than men.
This is as it has always been -
So all you need say is 'Amen'!

Why?

Why do pins, when you seek their head,
Always come up point instead?
And why must zippers always be
So awkward when you need to pee?
Why, when you leave a glass of wine
Do fruit flies fall in? (Rotten swine!)
And tell me why a fresh new shirt
Invariably attracts the dirt?
Why is it, when I clip my toes
I don't see where the off-cut goes?
And why, the way my moustache grows
Do stray hairs tickle on my nose?
Tell me why my neighbour's cat
Uses my garden to do 'that',
And why it is it's always pissed
On the tiny bit of ground I've missed?
And why, whenever soup you slurp
It always comes back as a burp?

Atchoo!

Nothing is worse than a man with a cold
Whether he's young or whether he's old.
He suffers much worse than all women born
And meets disbelief with uttermost scorn.
His nose is more blocked, his eyes water more;
He goes on about it - God! What a bore!

Water load of rubbish!

Timothy Sutton,
Bright as a button,
While working one day in his garden,
Said, 'It comes to mind
I simply must find
A whatsit.' I said, 'Beg your pardon?'
'You know what I mean
That thing with a stream
Of water at very high pressure.'
'A Karcher?' I said
Off the top of my head.
He said,' Nasty sneeze – ah, God bless yer!'
'Oh, Good Lord,' I sighed
As he thus replied,
' 'Tis merely the name you are after.
Karcher is German
You know – like Herman.'
'Gesundheit!' he said with much laughter.

Present fashions

With burgeoning bell-buttons
And tempting tums on view
It's enough to send boys crazy:
Oh golly! Jeepers! Phew!
But with all things considered
It is a better way.
I can only say I wish it
Had been like that in my day!

First and last – The mystery of Drax

Rain pours on the first day of term -
Ask the ladies and they'll confirm
That all their efforts made to clean
The floors and have a pristine gleam
Invariably are set at nought.
It really is a striking thought
How, through the school's long history,
There still remains the mystery:
Why is Commem Day fair and bright
While gloomy rain clouds heave in sight
And rain lies round in glistening pool
When boys and girls return to school?
Could the rain be the school-child's tear
Which greets the start of each new year,
While Commem says free time is nigh
And smiles replace the tearful sigh?

What if?

Wherefore art thou, Romeo?
Juliet has vertigo
Perched on balcony so high
Greeting lover with a sigh,
'Hurry Romeo! Be quick!
I am feeling mighty sick!'
God forbid that vomit cover
Th' upturned face of her poor lover!
What will Shakespeare find to say
When he comes to write the play?

Bonnie Scotland

Glorious days in Edinburgh town.
The streets went up and the rain came down,
The pavements sluiced and my head got wetter.
Would the damned weather never get better?
My knees both ached and my feet were sore,
I really thought I could take no more...
Then, when I was about to scream,
I woke to find it was a dream.
Through the window, morning light
Flooded in with sunshine bright.

Vive le Rosbif!

France played the All-Blacks yesterday
And, my word, didn't they make hay!
Les Francais, in without a chance,
Led New Zealand a merry dance.
No-one there gave the French a shout
And yet the All-Blacks were knocked out.
How was it that France won the match?
The answer's clear, there is no catch.
The reason is, 'tis my belief,
The French team all ate British Beef!

Fate

Why does an object choose to fall
Between the work-bench and the wall?
Why to retrieve that bloody screw
Must we all be subjected to
The acts of things inanimate
Whose goal is to exacerbate
The irritation we all know
When faced by the fatal blow
Of Sod's Law!

Cool, clear water

Let me pollute, since gain is all,
For what care I what may befall
All those who of clean water dream
Amid surroundings far downstream?
The problem's theirs, for I'll not pay
To clear my filthy muck away.

Water! Water!

A pee's
So wee
I cannot see
The necessity of flushing.
It's much too much
To thus send such
Amount of water rushing.

A fishy tale

Do catfish miaow, do dogfish still bark,
Do lobsters still dance the quadrille?
Are fishy affairs played out in the dark
Where they their love-life fulfil?

I fear that the fish will never be free
From man's overpowering greed.
The fishing boats skim the life from the sea
Without ever respecting their need.

And now, not content with fishing them out,
We rip up the sea-bed as well.
Just to give builders their gravel and grout
Marine life can just go to hell.

Dubbya

Now, George 'Dubbya' Bush, he comes out to play,
Asks, 'How can I f**k the world up today,
Now that already I have f****d it up
By attacking Iraq with Blair, my pup?'
His advisers say, 'Easy. Just refuse
To treat Palestinians as you treat the Jews.
That way you're certain to unleash the beast
Of Islamic hatred in the Middle East.'

C'est la Guerre

The echoes of the shot rebound.
The soldier falls without a sound.
His life seeps out upon the floor.
His wife, bereaved, will feel no more
His arms around her as before.

Why is it that mankind acts so?
How can it be he sinks so low?
Why is there always war and strife?
How can he take a precious life
And so deprive a loving wife?

Will it be that God will give
A time when man with man will live
In peace and perfect harmony?
When all from fear of war are free
And violent death is forced to flee?

Global Warming

Dubbya says, 'I'm for the *now* -
Not for what's to come.
To Kyoto I'll not bow -
And don't you call *me* dumb!

Recycling

Box for paper, box for plastic,
Box for dated things scholastic,
Box for bottles, box for tin,
Box for putting boxes in,
Box for bits and box for pieces,
Box for me when my life ceases.

Haiku

Summer now has come;
Autumn-tide will soon follow;
Winter will kill both.

One of those days

Oh! What a horrible morning!
Oh! What a horrendous day!
I've got a horrible feeling
Everything's going astray!

Oh no! Not again!

My dear, should we now end it all
Before the Third World War?
I do not think that, at our age,
We can put up with more.
We have, I know, the both of us
Been through it all before.
To find ourselves back there again
Would be an awful bore!

4

~ End of Work ~

When a man fell into his anecdotage it was a sign for him to retire from the world.

Benjamin Disraeli

Retirement is when you stop doing what you have to do and start doing what you want to do.

Anon

~ *End of Work* ~

Freedom

Sun-drenched mountains, hazy sea;
How sublime to feel so free;
No constraints to hold us back,
Thoughts are golden, never black.
Work, I fear, is but a fetter.
Retirement is so much better!

Aspects of Retirement

My wife cooks and bakes and sews,
Paints, embroiders, runs up clothes,
Works with ribbons, frills and bows,
Digs and rakes and plants and hoes,
Up and down all England goes,
Looks a treat from head to toes -

And I chop sticks!
(But I do it rather well!)

Beatitude

Blessed are the staff who can, each day,
Rise from their beds and straightway say.
'I want to teach.'
More blessed are those who can, each day,
Turn in their beds and straightway say,
'I want to sleep!

Postcards from Retirement

(each year after retiring, I sent a postcard to my ex-colleagues at Drax, extolling the pleasures of retirement – never, of course, gloating!
Only when I deemed few would remember me did my correspondence cease.)

Year 1

Come, lads and lasses, think of me
As I am sitting by the sea
And you are standing in your class
Surrounded by horrendous mass
Of minds obtuse and minds perverse
Enough to make a teacher curse!
Now, tell me straight and tell me true
That if the choice were up to you
Would you not rather be like me
And now be sitting by the sea?

Year 2

The life down here may well be rough
But there is sun and that's enough.
A pool to laze by through the day,
The sky above is blue, not grey.
Towns to visit, things to see,
And, above all, no 4C!
I know my nomenclature's wrong,
I've been away from Drax too long.
Had I remained at work, why then
I'd know that they are now 'Year Ten'.
Enjoy the term, fight the good fight -
I'll see you all on Concert night.

Year 3

This year, I'll be considerate
And try not to exacerbate
Your envy of my present state.
I will not ratiocinate
But merely say I find it great
To go to bed and get up late
Without the overbearing weight
Of doing all the things I hate.
To feel the sun upon my pate
While I my navel contemplate
And though I *can* ignore the date
I'll join you to Commemorate!

Year 4

What's there to say?
A lovely day
And I'm making hay
While the sun shines.

To be quite fair
I wouldn't dare
To declare
That my heart pines

To see masses
Of classes
All seeking passes
At exam times.

Year 5

Nice and *Nice*
Like *pies* and *peas*
Go well together
Just as *lovely* and *weather*.

Menton has *bon ton*
And Grasse has class.
St Tropez is okay
While Vintimiglia is famiglia
To those who
Go thro'
Seeking better times
In foreign climes.

All in all
I'm having a ball
Taking 'the cure'
On the Cote d'Azur.

Year 6
(To Sandra Fanning, who was the Headmaster's P.A.)

Oh! Mrs Fanning
While I'm here tanning
My back in the sun
And having fun,
You're there at Drax
Dispatching fax,
Keeping your nerve
And all your verve,
Despite the hassle
Of having to wrestle
With people who
Keep pestering you
With silly rhymes
From foreign climes.

Year 7

Sandra – be not Cassandra.
Be of good cheer – Uncle Mac is here
To bring you fun – and a hint of sun
And happy times – from foreign climes.

Year 8

R.I.P.

Come raise a cheer for 'tis the last.
The days of gloating are now past,
For others soon will join my state
And have just cause to celebrate.
I'll hand to them Calliope's banner
And let them emulate my manner.
My lyric muse must now be still
And silenced now my rhyming skill.
I'll play no more the poetaster
Content to be an ex-schoolmaster.

Or

I promise you 'twill be my last.
The time for gloating is now past,
For others soon will join my state -
They, too, can freedom celebrate.
Let them their rhyming talents test
While I retire to well-earned rest.
I'll cease to be a poetaster
And merely be an ex-schoolmaster.

5

~ *Play up! Play up!* ~

Playing snooker gives you firm hands and helps build up character. It is the ideal recreation for dedicated nuns.

Luigi Barbarito
(The Pope's emissary, attending a sponsored snooker tournament at Tyburn Abbey)

Some people think football is a matter of life and death...
I can assure them it is much more serious than that.

Bill Shankly

~ Play up! Play up! ~

Fishin' at Drax

It's a funny owd game is this 'anglin' -
Yer sits on a bank wi' a stick,
Yer bait is in t' watter a-danglin'.
No wonder folk think that yer thick.

Yer sits there all day and yer catch nowt,
Yer pack up yer things and go back,
Yer say to yersen, 'Ah know nowt about owt,
Ah think I'll go ask Uncle Mac.'

'Nay, nay, niver come and ask me, lad.
Ah know less than thee, so they say.
As an angler Ah allus wor reet bad
An' Ah'm gettin' wus ivry day.

Ah've tried ivry which way to catch some
Wi' waggler and still-watter blue,
But Ah've never managed to land one,
Nay, nay, lad, Ah 'aven't a clue!

If tha' wants to catch fish at Brock'oles
Tha'll 'ave ter ask them down at t'club.
They'll show thee 'ow to use t'roach-pole
And 'appen 'ow to land chub.

But if tha end up empty-'anded.
Don't think o' thissen as a fool.
Just say ter thissen (and be candid)
'It's better ner stoppin' i' school!'

Golfin'

It's a funny owd game is this golfin'.
Yer 'it a white ball wi' a stick,
Yer send it all which-ways a-flyin' -
No wonder folks think that yer thick.

Yer tek out an iron and bash it
But the divot flies further than t'ball.
Three more goes! Nay, lad, it's the limit,
You really are no good at all.

Yer spend more time searchin' in t'bunker
Fer balls that you've struck out o' sight
Disturbin' the sparrers and thrushes,
Gi'in' them an almighty fright.

Yer reach the last green – and the club'ouse -
The members watch you putt for t'hole.
Four putts and all miss – now they can grouse -
T'green looks t'have been 'it by a mole.

A notice goes up in the bar-room:
A trolley and all clubs for sale.
There's nobbut one thing I can assume -
That is, yer were destined to fail!

Hacker's Golf

A greater joy has the hacker
Than even the very best pro,
For he has the infinite pleasure
Of the one immaculate blow.
For him, the one in a hundred
Is better than six under par,
Since he has no reason to wonder
If ever he could get that far.

De Amico Amato – In Memoriam – Vale Wolsey

Come good folks all and grieve with me
For Arthur, driving from the tee
Saw not where his dear ball had flown,
And his companions, forced to own
That they had failed to see its flight,
Had added greatly to his plight.
How could he lose his trusty friend?
It could not be! Heaven forfend!
But Wolsey, which, day in, day out,
Had well withstood his Yorkshire clout,
Had sailed away through sunlit air,
And fell to earth, one knew not where.
They all set to, searched high and low
To no effect. Ah me! Oh, woe!
But Arthur did not long stay blue;
He now plays with a Masters 2!

World Match Play 2001

Woosie doo'd it after all this time!
He found the distance and found the line.
With quick appreciation and effortless swing
He clawed back all lost ground – hey ding a-ding ding!
How nice to see the oldie make his way back.
Neither skill nor perseverance does he lack.

Snooker

It's a funny owd game is this snooker;
Yer hits a white ball wi' a stick.
Yer miss nearly all t'shots that yer go fer -
No wonder folks think that yer thick.

Yer play all neet long and yer win nowt.
Yer pack up yer cue and go back.
Yer say to yersen, 'Ah know nowt about owt,
Ah'm afraid that Ah'm losin' the knack!'

At snooker Ah used ter be reet good
But Ah'm getting' wus ivry day.
Ah'm off to end up as a reet dud
Fightin' 'ard to keep despair at bay.

Ah've tried ivry which way to pot some
Wi' stun, wi' checkside and wi' screw,
But Ah niver manage to pot one -
Nay, nay, lads, Ah 'aven't a clue!

Ah think Ah'll come in just to watch it
An' sit wi' a pint in the gloom
An' consider 'ow Ah 'ave botched it -
Allus t'usher and niver the groom.

Beaten on the Black

You struggled, Gordon, but in vain;
None of the joy, but all the pain.
Back I came after three weeks' rest;
Managed (but how?) to come out best.
The victor by a fearful fluke -
Enough to make a good man puke!
But, though you must have felt aghast,
Admit – I saved the best till last!

Don't tell Dennis

(to the tune of Don't bring Lulu)

You can fluke a blue
With an old bent cue
But don't tell Dennis.

If how you sink a pink
Would drive him to drink,
Don't tell Dennis.

Dennis is the kind of man
Who likes a game to go to plan
So he's apt to wear a frown
When it's luck that pots the brown.

If your biggest break
Starts with a mistake
Then don't tell Dennis.

Should the ball be struck
With a deal of pot-luck
It all becomes too much.

Another fluking smarty
Who ruins our Den's party.
He's a real menace.
Don't tell Dennis -
He'll tell you himself!

(If you fluke on Dennis, get ready to duck,
For he plays with skill, whereas you play with luck!)

King Arthur

Tuesday night at the Bowling Club and Arthur's back in town.
The other snooker players blench; they know the chips are down.
For Arthur is a mean player. If he can't pot the ball,
He takes good care to put it safe and leave them naught at all.
When he walks in, the crowds all thin as he takes out his cue.
They know full well he'll sink them all: the reds, the black, the blue.
He improved as the time went by, like wine in bottle lying.
He eyed a shot, lined it up and sent the balls a'flying.
He says he is not now so good as once he used to be,
Yet I say who, with a bent cue, can make a fifty-three?
But you know that o'er the years the killer instincts soften.
King Arthur still can beat the lads – just not quite so often.

Snookered or Lumb<u>a</u>red?

A fortnight I've been gone – too long!
Pray listen to my plaintive song.
For all week long I've staggered round,
To feeble movement I've been bound.
But yet I've come to play 'gainst thee
Where, weekly, I am deemed to be.
As here my painful back I bend
And (hopefully) I try to send
The ball I strike to pocket,
(I fear I'll need a larger bucket!0
Please, at my efforts do not sneer
But praise those shots that get quite near.

Tim's Team at Wembley?

Hoorah! Hooray! We've done the biz!
Our football team was full of fizz!
We finally made the buggers yield
And saw off plucky Chesterfield.
What remains for Middlesborough
Is to go and make a thorough
Success of our final hurdle:
May our fancy footwork curdle
Skills and courage of poor Chelsea
So that Bryan's team wins, else he
May find that because of lack
Of silverware he'll get the sack.
Bosses are not esteemed merely
For achieving only *nearly.*
Let's hope and pray May brings reward
With F.A. Cup on the sideboard.

(But if they at this hurdle fell
Then life with Tim would be pure hell!)

Smile, Tim, Smile

Just to prove they've been on song,
Rarely putting a foot wrong,
Winning well all season long,
'Borough's back where they belong.

After last year's minor blip,
They're now set to make the trip
To the very topmost tip
Of the football Premiership.

Either that or next year, too,
Tim is doomed to feeling blue
As their season goes askew
With demotion's bitter brew.

Tim's Traumatic Travels

'I went up to 'Borough the other day
Went up to 'Borough to see my team play
And there, mercy me, to my utter dismay
The other team playing did show mine the way.
The opposing side, by name Bradford City,
Had a style of play that was nought if not gritty.
At the end of the game – ah me! What a pity! -
They'd stuffed us one-nil! Oh well, mate, tough titty!

Round Four
(Middlesborough 2 – Manchester United 0)

Who's a happy boy, then, this wet and windy day?
Middlesborough showed Man United how to play.
Two-nil to the blues (even though they played in red).
The grey/white clad United should have stayed in bed.
Now what lies in store for them as fourth round draws near?
If they play like that again, then there's nowt to fear.
Only win a few more rounds – keep your peckers up -
And you could be proud winners of the F.A. Cup.

The Cup Quarter-Finals

There you are, I told you so -
The lads have done it again.
You can sit there all a-glow;
They won without any pain.
They have a semi-final place.
Your hopes are rising higher.
They only need themselves to pace
And play with guts and fire.
One more round and it's your hope
That they'll be in the final
And if they are and if they cope,
Then, Tim, I'll say that mine'll
Be a pint on you!

Bugger! Borough Beaten!

It was the cruellest fate of all
That Festa should have put the ball
In his own net.
It therefore means that not at all
Will 'Borough grace the Final Ball -
Still – ne'er mind, pet!

Owzat!

It's a funny owd game is this cricket;
Yer 'its a red ball wi' a stick.
Yer spend t'day defendin' yer wicket -
No wonder folks think that yer thick.

A fella comes up an' 'e's runnin',
'E throws the red ball at yer stick.
'E throws it wi' such skill and cunnin'
That yer out. Bugger off – an' be quick!

Yer spend all next day in t'pavilion
While t'others 'ave t'chance to use t'stick.
The men runnin' round are vermilion,
Chasin' balls as 'ave come from a snick.

Then, after four days, t'game is over.
Yer pack up yer gear an' go 'ome
And after all t'fuss an' all t'bother
Yer sit down an' write this 'ere pome!

Tennis

Now, I have a theory about lawn tennis.
That is: The first service holds far less menace
Than the second serve which, softly delivered,
Leaves the opponent completely bewildered.
The second serve, softer, seems to gain the point
And thus puts the opponent's nose out of joint.
Why, when it is fizzing and fast, does it fail,
Whereas slow and gentle gets you out of jail?
The answer is simple – Forget your first serve,
Use your second to get the point you deserve.

6

~ *Il faut cultiver notre jardin* ~

Cela est bien dit, repondit Candide, mais il faut cultiver notre jardin.
(Well said, replied Candide, but our garden needs tending.)

Voltaire

When you get down to it, as sooner or later you must, gardening is a long-drawn-out war of attrition against the elements, a tripartite agreement involving the animal, insect and bird worlds, and the occasional sheer perversity of Nature.

Alan Melville

~ Il faut cultiver notre jardin ~

The Joys of gardening

Polygonum or Russian Vine -
An all-pervasive rotten swine!
Whate'er you do, for all I whit,
There is no way of stopping it.
Stand nowhere near it, please, I beg,
Or 'twill be up your trouser leg,
Around your neck, your ears, your face,
Invading every bit of space.
Naught can stop its bold advance.
Prune it? Joking! Not a chance!
Medusa-like it writhes and wreathes
With bobbing leaves and tendrils seethes.
For every shoot that's cut away
Three more grow by end of day.
I shall resort to dynamite
To put an end to this dire blight,
For that's the only way, it's plain,
To get my garden back again!

Spuggies

A profligate bird is the sparrow -
Homes in on the feed like an arrow.
It's beak is precise;
Its feet, not so nice,
Scatter seed from Bristol to Barrow.

The Joys of Gardening II

Spring-Summer long I wield my shears,
Clipping, curtailing, curbing years
Of over-long, luxuriant growth,
Legacy of idle gardener's sloth,
Until, at last, a solid sheen
Of hard-won, small leaves, glowing green,
Meets my gaze as, proud, I see
The neatness that I've brought to be.
So it is with great relief
I contemplate my small, neat leaf.

But lo! In Winter's icy blast
My efforts of the summer past
Are surely not destined to last,
For now a host of sparrows fly
In criss-cross flutter that my eye
Is now too old to well espy.
Feeding-time at the bird table,
Plummeting from nearby gable,
They now prove that they are able
To penetrate my well-cut hedge
And carve themselves a precious ledge
Whence, perched securely on the edge,
They can watch for any danger,
Acting as their comrades' ranger
Darting down to avine manger.

Sadly, each time that they dart
Into my hedge, they tear apart
My hours of toil, my work of art.
But, though I shed a little tear,
I can repair it, never fear,
By working hard at it next year.
So feed in safety all day long,
Eat your seed and sing your song
Snug in my hedge, where you belong.

Feed the birds, tuppence a day!

About birds there is one thing
I have noticed – that they fling
The seeds and feed that I provide
To the four winds, far and wide.
They always seem to eat their fill
And yet they seem as much to spill.
So, as I'm looking all around,
I find as much spread on the ground
As that which I placed in their tin.
It seems to me profligate sin
To scatter thus their food supply
Which I provide so they get by
When times are hard and weather cold,
When eyesight's poor and wings are old.
But I suppose 'twas ever thus
So I've no call to make a fuss.

The joys of gardening III

Escallonia
And Mahonia
Don't mix -
Mahonia pricks!

The winter wind *is* unkind.

Now, why is it when I, with zest
Am sweeping leaves towards the West,
That the wind blows, without the least
Thought for my needs, straight from the East?
Straightforward logic must then rule:
Go with the flow, you silly old fool!

The Dainty Dunnock

What does a Dunnock think about?
Hops around with ne'er a shout.
In and out the hedge-row goes,
Never treads on others' toes.
Never joins in sparrows' rowing,
Always to their squabbles bowing.
Feeds upon what they let fall
While fighting, but not at all
Worried by the fight above.
Hops with shadows hand in glove,
Leads its little, quiet life.
Goes home, tranquil, to its wife.

Autumn Leaves

The other day at dawning,
Greeted by a windless morning,
I decided to sweep up the fallen leaves.
I got them nicely sorted;
Then my efforts were aborted,
Enough to make any gardener grieve.
The slight wind which had gone down
Came gently back to play the clown
And distributed my leaves both far and wide.
Sweeping downwind didn't help
For, like some sea-borne kelp,
They fluttered on the path from side to side.

Whatever the time, whatever the day,
The wind always blows the opposite way!

The Joys of Gardening IV

The shrub Pyrocantha, or Firehorn -
The cussedest plant that ever was born,
To my way of thinking! It has the knack
Of first growing up and then turning back.
From left hand to right, it writhes and it wreathes,
Mingling dread thorns amongst flowers and leaves.
Its sweet-smelling blossoms bee-swarms attract,
Its autumnal fruits are by birds attacked.
Of trying to tame it I've had my fill;
It grows as it wants to, it grows at will.
I'll never admit it's better than me!
I *will* control its exuberant glee!
I've now cut it down right to ground level,
There, that'll show it, spiky old devil!
Damn! I've just looked at it – it's sprouting free,
The truncated stump will soon be a tree!
I'll lay down my saw and admit defeat –
It's stronger than me; to cede is quite meet.

Crumbs from the table

Down below small sparrows hop
Searching for the seeds that drop
From the table far above
Scattered by the greedy dove.

Rough Rhyme for Rosemary

Ah! Rosemary you stood, before
Your early death, at my back door,
But now, to make enough room for
A building of two rooms or more,
Untimely ripped from your roots now
You found yourself obliged to bow.
So here I promise, nay, I vow
Another place will I endow -
Ah, yes indeed, I will find room
For Rosemary once more to bloom.

Old Gardeners

The fact that Gardeners don't grow old
But instead go to pot
Worries me not one tittle
Nor even one small jot.
For if I can go thus to pot
I'll have a place to pittle!

7

~ *Family and Friends* ~

Children don't know better as they grow older; they merely know more.

Saki

I am a hoarder of two things: documents and trusted friends.

Muriel Spark

~ *Family and Friends* ~

Hyperactivity

My wife went up to bed last night
But half way there, she had a fright.
Lo and behold, upon the stair,
Another person she met there.
But, as the other one drew near,
She noticed something passing queer:
On looking at the face, she saw
That it was one she'd seen before.
In fact, it was the one she'd seen
On each occasion that she'd been
Using the mirror in her room
As she sat there herself to groom...
And suddenly to her occurred
The meaning of the words she'd heard:
'If you persist in rising soon,
Afore the setting of the moon,
Remember well what I have said -
You'll meet yourself going to bed!'

What? More?

You've had tables and pictures
And clothes and a car,
Fine animal carpets
And gifts from afar.
Now the shirt off my back
And the vest from my bum.
Is there aught else you'd ask for
From me and your Mum?
If there is, then don't falter,
Just ask us, please do -
It gives us great pleasure
To do things for you.

On my brother's spelling

Though my knowledge of grammar is limited
From my time spent at school I benefited.
When a word ends in 't'
Primal stress rules, you see.,
So the past tense of *rivet* is *riveted*

Getting my own back

Dearest daughter, mildly mocking,
Making fun of poor old Dad
With his poetastic rhyming,
Hinting that it's more than bad.
Vengeance is a dish best eaten
When it sits there icy cold.
I'll show her that I'm not beaten -
She'll read this until she's old!
On and on with time unfurling
Like some never-ending road
Filled with verses so toe-curling
She'll regret she ever sowed
Those small seeds of criticism
Of my efforts to divert,
Denigrating witticisms
Using words designed to hurt.
In return, with glee ferocious,
I'll confirm her darkest fears
Writing verse that's so atrocious
It will reduce her to tears!

The moral? You know it!
Don't mess with a poet!

To my grand-daughter
(who refused to kiss her granddad until she was nearly nine)

Oh1 Come on, Sam, give your papa a kiss.
You have so many that you'll never miss
One for a bearded, bald-headed old fellow.
Just one on the cheek will make him feel mellow.
You've managed to duck it for nigh-on nine years
And during that time you've reduced him to tears.
Just think of him having the kind of grand-daughter
Who, in giving kisses, don't do what she oughter!

Vanessa

Vanessa is a lovely child
And always seems so sunny.
Not that she is meek and mild
Even when she's funny.
She stops others running wild
Sometimes short of money!
And is always there when dialled -
What a lovely bunny!

To Laura

I thank you for your daisy chain
For, seeing it, it is quite plain
That you have spent a lot of time
To make it for me, and so I'm
Writing you this little note
Which would not get, I fear, the vote
Of anyone who likes good verse
(His comments would be rather terse!)
But if my rhyme amuses you
And makes *you* happy, that will do.

Saunders' Farewell

(Saunders was an 'invisible friend' created by my brother – responsible for many situations and activities not always socially acceptable!)

Saunders called on me today
With plaintive, tearful look, to say
He'd sent you greetings long ago
But answer there was none and so
He'd come to me to see if I
Could give to him the reason why
His card to you had been ignored.
I told him that I thought you bored
And, like some Doctor Frankenstein,
You now considered it was time
To get rid of your creation
Figment of imagination.

He wiped a teardrop from his eye
And answered me with mournful sigh:
'From earth we come and from dry dust
And back to them return we must.
But still I find it hard to go
And so I weep and mop and mow
That I must quit this earth so fair
Without my ever being there!'

Vanessa's Violin

'Vanessa's violin is here,
Just ring the school and you will hear
What you've to do and what to pay
And details of collection day.'

I've had a thought – Oh yes! I say!
Will Van-Van be another Mae?
Will people soon be all a-queuin'
To hear a blossoming Menuhin?
If it is so, that's really wild -
A musically gifted child!

David's Snowman

I once made a snowman – he stood on the lawn.
The weather turned warmer and then he was gone.
But where has he gone to – I *would* like to know,
This man who just stood there all covered in snow.
I feel, as he melted, some sank through the earth
And came back in flowers – a kind of re-birth.
The bees came for nectar, then flew to the hive,
So part of my snowman is still there alive.
The rest of him rose as light dew in the air.
The winds came and took him to spread everywhere.
He fell to the earth as sweet life-giving rain,
And so my old snowman is living again -
His arm's in Tibet and his head's in Peru
While his left leg is lying in wild Timbuctu.
His arm is a stream, his head is a flower,
The parts of his body all have the power
To refresh the earth and give people pleasure.
And, when it freezes, the children at leisure
Can pack the snow hard and then fashion the ice
And here he is back again and oh, that is nice!

Richard – Computer game King

King of computer games, knows all the tricks;
The eye cannot follow as his finger flicks
Over controls that he uses like braille.
He's no need to see them for he'll never fail
To push the button when he wants to score;
By zapping his foes he just makes room for more!
Down the long hall-way and then up the stair -
Now what's round that corner? An enemy's there!
Lightning reaction – the button is pressed.
To see that one off is not really a test!
The end of the game, and up comes the score -
The winner! By many a hundred, and more!
His skill is quite awesome – I wish that he could
Succeed in his schoolwork with scores just as good!

To Laura on winning Best Gown at the Ball

So, my dear, you now can see
There was no need for misery.
Like Cinderella at the Ball
You gained the greatest prize of all.
The gown you wore – adjudged the best -
Must, you'll admit, put to the test
That what you pay is the be-all
And end-all of your Prom'nade Ball.

Katie's hat

I adore a
Fedora.
But, meseems,
That blue jeans
Give no street-cred
To what's on your head.
But what know I of fashion?
Of youth it is the passion
And I'm too old
To be so bold
As to advance criticism
Through doggerel witticism.

Great Grandfather-hood

It seems I'm a great grandfather
Since my grandchildren tell the truth.
The times they tell me, 'O rather!
You're great, grandfather!' - there's the proof.
My great-granddaughter is too young;
Time will pass till the song is sung:
'You're really great, great-grandfather'!

Bank of (Grand)dad

I got the hint-
You need a mint
Of money to sustain her!
Now don't refuse,
I've more to use
To keep me and your mother!
But I've not got
The other lot
To reach the sum aspired.
I'll try, my dear
To give, next year,
The sum that you desired!

In Vino Veritas?
(addressed to an aspiring binge-drinker)

I may be an old fogey or be an old fart
But what I have to say comes direct from the heart:
You are still young and have a great deal to lose;
Don't give yourself up to consumption of booze.
If it is to get drunk that you take a drink,
It's time to step back, to consider and think.
You are intelligent – you don't lack brains.
A person like you is one who refrains
From excessive intake, who reflects on his acts
And is quick to acknowledge the truth of the facts.

Little Miss Harriet

Little Miss Harriet,
No need to marry yet.
Plenty of time to get
A nice young man.
But if you've had enough
Of finding dross and rough,
Why not take Christopher -
A nice young man?

Thanks to David who cut my grass

He who labours on a Sunday
Merits a refreshing drink.
You may, or not, agree with me
But that is what *I* think.
To find my grass trimmed neatly
(Better by far than my beard!)
Means he who was responsible
Deserves to be revered.
(And so does she, I have a hunch,
Who laboured long to cook your lunch!)

To Maureen

Maureen – (That's Mo)
Can sing high and low
Full of pizazz
When the song's jazz;
Writes poetry and plays
In so many ways;
Paints with the best
And knows how to jest.
I honestly would
Be like her, if I could.

The Bare facts *or* The Naked Truth

Forgive me Jill if I seem rude
But I have seen you in the nude.
'Twas on the beach of Scarborough fair
With all its gusting, freezing air
That your mother, my Auntie Phyl,
Undressing you with little skill
Left you, naked, standing there
Exposed to cold, and curious stare.
Of course, by now, it's history
But to me was shown the mystery
Of how the ladies and the men
Are not the same. (To that – Amen!)
Shocked was I to see nothing there
While I was blessed with hose and pair.

8

~ *Words, Words, Words* ~

Polonius: *What do you read, my lord?*
Hamlet: *Words, words, words.*

William Shakespeare

Serendipity means searching for a needle in a haystack and instead finding a farmer's daughter.

Anon

~ *Words, words, words* ~

Just write a poem

'Just write a poem,' the master said,
But, when I tried, my muse had fled.
I sat alone and racked my brain
In vain!

'Just write a poem.' 'Twas said with ease.
Ideas hopped round my brain like fleas.
But when it comes to pen and ink –
Can't think!

'Just write a poem.' I gave a groan.
On my resources I was thrown.
Because of this my brows I knit.
No wit!

'Just write a poem.' What a task!
'Tis more than any man should ask,
Reducing those of tender years
To tears!

'Just write a poem.' I beg to state
Because of this I sat up late.
Until my mother sternly said,
'To bed!'

What skill?

A certain ability with facile rhyme
Helps me fill my retired time.
Rhyming couplets drip and fall
With no artistic worth at all.
From time to time, a rhyme more vile
Brings, as reward, a fleeting smile.

My father – 'Mad Acko' as he was known – was Head of Classics at Nunthorpe Grammar School, where he drummed into me and many other boys the essentials of Latin and Greek.

Some sixty years later, I still find myself reading with the echoes of my father still in my head, his explanations of the derivation of words as apposite now as when he first expressed them.

Somnium

Last night I dreamed in Latin throughout my troubled sleep.
Ablatives were absolute; my slumber-tide was neap!
Trapped was I *intra muros* and I could not define
Which verb, among the many, I needed to decline.
Excalibur tripped through my mind – I'd hack my way out!
But I recalled *exeo* – released with joyful shout!
Through many hours of darkness, I was subjected to
The case of *direct object* – *(accusative* to you.)
The supine behaved itself and lived up to its name.
Participles, Past and Present, also did the same.
A night of Classic action, to make my father proud.
On waking, '*Ave Pater'* was what I said aloud.

Measure for Measure

Is the battle lost or won?
Less or *fewer*? Choose the one
That best suits the cogent case.
Let us, as a nation, face
The fact that we seem not to know
If we're reckoning part or whole.
Less relates to part or bits -
Fewer links to whole units.

Omnibus

What is it that approaches us?
Why, surely, it's an omnibus.
I stand at the kerb and say,
'Veni! Veni! O omnibe!'
Ah, yes, I'm sure – I see it come.
At last we have an *omnibum.*
Am I correct in what I see?
The back end of an *omnibi?!*
I can't catch it! I shall show
My deep disgust to this *omnibo.*
If only it was crawling slow
I could leap on this *omnibo.*
An omnibus, then *omnibi* -
You wait for one, then there are three!
They follow one another – see?
Come forth, elusive *omnibi*!
I see them in a huddle close,
Those intermittent *omnibos.*
And so, at last, we have a quorum
Of red-hued London *omniborum.*
I give a sneer to all of these,
To swarming, clustered *omnibis.*
By, with, from, in, on, at – O cease! -
All words to use with *omnibis.*
I say, crudely, 'Up your jacksie!
I'm off, mate – to take a taxi!'

In Brevitate Veritas

It's easy when you write rubbish.
It's when you write well that it's hard.
It's with poor rhymes that I flourish;
I write them all day by the yard!

Declining Love

I Perfect

Amabo, amabis
She'll give me a kiss.
Amabit, amabamus,
She'll make a pair of us
Amabitis, amabunt,
With love abundant. *

II Imperfect

Amabam, amabas
She's dropped me, alas!
Amabat, amabamus,
Ah me! What bad traumas!
Amabatis, amabant,
I can but rave and rant.

III Past Perfect

Amavi, amavisti
We are no longer frisky!
Amavit, amavimus,
Now, why was there all that fuss?
Amavisti, amaverunt,
Thank God I'm not a parent!*

*(Yes, I know other rhymes suggest themselves -
but you shouldn't be thinking words like that!)*

Thin Skin

The inability to accept criticism
Even in the form of witticism
Is a failing common to
Many among us who
Should know better
That to let a
Piece of advice
Turn us to ice.

Three cheers for Doggerel

All I have is a way with words,
To which your answer is: 'Absurd's
The word that I would rather choose
To qualify the awful use
Of rhyming couplets' rise and fall -
Poetically, bugger-all!'
And yet, in my timid defence,
I claim that they give no offence
To those who find it hard to see
The sense in 'modern' poetry.

Poetry as Therapy

You may well quite abhor it.
You may well quite ignore it,
But when all is said and done,
Poetry is so much fun.
And, whatever you may say,
It keeps Alzheimer's at bay.

Long Live bad Rhymesters!

I can't give up my doggerel.
I can't eschew my lambent rhyme.
I crow like some young cockerel
And strive so hard to keep in time.
I tread a tightrope, oh so fine,
To keep rhythm within each line.
You may well judge the result sad
But it keeps me from going mad.
So it's 'Long live all bad rhymesters!'
And 'Away with all Alzheimers!'

9

~ Bons Anniversaires ~

*Happy Birthday to you,
Squashed tomatoes and stew,
Bread and butter in the gutter,
Happy birthday to you.*

Anon

*Tomorrow is our wedding-day
And we will then repair
Unto the Bell at Edmonton
All in a chaise and pair.*

William Cowper

~ Bons Anniversaires ~

David's tenth

Dear David, if you were called Len
Or carried the Christian name Ken
I'd find it much easier when
Sitting here in my little den
I'm sucking the end of my pen
Seeking words that will rhyme with TEN!

Laura's Tenth birthday

Said One to Nought, 'I'm better than you.
Since I'm in front, it must be true'
Said Nought to One, 'That's not the line,
Since you're worth one and I'm worth nine.'
Said One to Nought, 'How does that figure?'
Said Nought to One, 'I make you bigger.
I'm worth nine; you, one; so then
Add nine to one and you've got ten!'

Samantha's thirteenth

Well, now that you're a *teenie*
A 'twixt and in-betweenie,
I fear life will not always be quite fair.
Your body may grow lumpy,
Your parents will be grumpy,
Your requests will be greeted by a glare.
So, your face may grow some zits,
You may think school is the pits,
And greasiness may lanken your limp hair.
But there's one thing that's for sure:
For all this there is a cure -
It's TIME! And you'll get better. Ah! There, there!
For, when all is said and done,
It's a battle you'll have won
Since you'll still be Samantha – *avis rare!*

What! Another?

You're thirty-one?
        but don't be glum.
No, never fear –
        life's not all dun.
Though daughter's doubt
        and son's tantrum
May make you wish
        you'd been a nun.
Though layers of fat
        on bum and tum
May make you feel
        you weigh a ton.
It's not all bad –
        there's years to come
Of joy and pleasure
        laughs and fun,
Of husband, kids
        and me and Mum.
Why, think again!
        Life's just begun!

Plus One

Another year, another wrinkle
But only when the laugh-lines crinkle.
A birthday? Now, no need to holler,
No need to heat up 'neath the collar.
Just think, you could be forty-three
But I'm quite sure that you'll agree
How old you feel is up to you
So here's a toast to ?????-two!

My Wife's Birthday

I couldn't let your birthday pass
Without writing for you, my lass,
Just one more time
A simple rhyme.
I'll search my mind for one more way
In which I can truthfully say
That all the years are far too few
To show my feelings, dear, for you.
I've tried in vain this year to find
A way to say what's in my mind;
I think the simplest way is best -
Je t'aime – so is my love expressed.

Forty Years On

I'm sorry, dear, I really tried.
I sucked my pen, scratched head and sighed,
But yet I fear no rhymes would come.
For once, I was completely dumb.
The rhyming couplets failed to fall.
I'd no poetic skill at all.
I feel that, all in all, the lack
Of ode is down to my bad back.
I fear the pain just took away
Awareness of th' important day.
I did ring but was forced to keep
All my good wishes – beep!beep!beep!
But still, with you I must agree
The fact that you are now forty
Is worthy of a little rhyme
Though I am somewhat behind time.
So, here's to forty, here's to you,
Do not be saddened, don't be blue.
Go to Dublin, look for Molly.
Take a rest and have a jolly!

The Allotted Span
(To my brother on his 70th birthday)

At last it's three score years and ten.
So what is it that you do then?
If you are godly, do you say,
'I've had my lot – I'll go away
And shuffle off this mortal coil,
Leaving all others here to toil'?
Or, being human, do you say,
'I'll live to fight another day'
Since, if you go, you cannot tell
Whether you'll find yourself in Hell?
The purgatory of life is so
Much better than hell-fire below.

To Betty at 80

Now at last the immovable object
Must give way to irresistible force!
I'll certainly come to your eightieth -
Such a great day is sacrosanct, of course.
But, above all, don't ask for a poem -
My powers are failing me day by day.
As our Rabbie Burns said, long before me,
Plans of mice, men (and poets) gang aglay.
Not only have my lines gone uneven;
Faced with all this, I am sure you'll agree,
My lines, like Rab's plan, are lop-sided,
Not only aglay but also aglee!

Birthday books

Books this year are all the rage
Giving me page after page
Of quiet, peaceful pleasure
To be enjoyed at leisure.
From epic tale to lighter jokes,
To one who resolutely pokes
Fun at those whose punctuation
Breeds, in her, exasperation.
I know the feeling well, I fear.
From time to time, I shed a tear
As *fewer* gives up ground to *less*
And grammar ends up in a mess.
They've all brought back to me the cheer
Of Birthdays, Christmas, yesteryear.
When I was asked to say what took
My fancy, I replied, 'A book!'
E'en when I'm older – let us say
Twenty more years from today -
Then, truly, 'tis not my belief
That I'll wish for a handkerchief.
Indeed, to linen, I do think
That I prefer good printers' ink.

Birthday verse for my wife

I looked all over for a card;
Both high and low I looked quite hard.
But cards these days are mostly rude
(In fact, they can be awfully crude).
Where are the cards of yesteryear
That tell one that one holds one dear?
You'll have to make do with this bear
So you can once more this year share
My thoughts as I wake up with you -
That I love you, I truly do.

Ruby Wedding
(to a relative who sent a card early)

I know rubies are red, and sapphires are blue,
That I am forgetful – but, then, so are you.
To receive our card thirty days before time
Made me stop – and think – and then wonder – if I'm
All wrong in my dates. Had we wed in July?
That *may* be the case – but then I'm convinced I
Got married in France some time after that
(If my memory's wrong, I'll just eat my hat.)
Twenty-sixth of July was when *you* got wed;
Just one week later to the Mairie I led
Sylviane, who has suffered long for her pains -
Ask her if the losses have outweighed the gains!
Of course, simple reason can explain the date -
You were simply determined not to be late!

(You've had fourteen lines – that makes it a sonnet;
I'll put my pen down now – no more comment on it.)

50th Anniversary

There really is no better way
Than doggerel to mark the day,
So I propose that, if I may,
I will go on singing my lay,
Employing rotten rhymes to say
How well you've kept the years at bay.
Long may the sunshine's golden ray
Fall upon you as you make hay
And let no-one say me nay
As I say 'Happy Golden Day!'

(Fifty is 'L' – but not for you -
Life together is a sweeter brew!)

Wonders never cease

How has she done it?
How can it be?
O'er fifty years
She's put up with me!
I can not say more
How much I adore
The lady who lies by my side.
My doggerel life
Deserves not a wife
Who with me can so long abide.

50th Anniversary – and more!

I'm proud to see my love grow old,
To see the jaw-line soften,
To see the lines about her mouth,
To see the laugh-line crinkles show,
To see the proud breast tip-tilt go,
To see the tiny wasp-waist grow.
Should I go on, for I've seen all?
I've spent my loving years with her
And, to my joy, she's with me still
Despite my faults – greater than hers.
I love her and I stand amazed
At intellectual sharpness shown
For interests, both far and wide:
Wife, mother, artist, teacher, chef,
Manager in my fallen state.
In Heaven's name, what more to ask?
I've been in Heaven for so long.
And, God, I wish my life to last
A few days less than her life-span.

10

~ All Year Round ~

Never sign a Valentine with your own name.

Sam Weller (in Dickens' *Pickwick Papers*)

And girls in slacks remember Dad
And oafish louts remember Mum
And sleepless children's hearts are glad,
And Christmas-morning bells say 'Come!'

John Betjeman

~ All Year Round ~

New Year's Eve 2002

Goodbye Two Thousand and Two,
We've all seen enough of you.
Hello, Two Thousand and Three,
Take your place in history.
Reveal what is in store ahead -
How many millions will be dead
From man's unthinking interactions
Of too many fighting factions
Led by men too conscious of
Their own importance, not their love
Or pity for those others who
Have no choice but to do
What they are told.

Valentine I

I think this year it is high time
That I named you my Valentine.
Thirty-six years now have flown
Since I first made you my own,
Yet to my undying shame
Never have I put your name
Upon a card! Enough of that,
I'll make amends at last, *ma chatte.*

Valentine II

Virtue is its own reward
All the sages say.
Love is said to conquer all
Especially today.
Now is the time for tender men
To plight their troth anew.
I do it now as once before -
New pledged am I to you.

Valentine III

If I send you flowers divine,
If I give you chocolates fine,
If I chill you fine white wine,
If I take you out to dine,
If I say for you I pine,
If I declare that I am thine -
Then will you be my Valentine?

Valentine IV

Fourteenth of February! Here again!
Through many a year have you sought in vain
To finally find out who is the swain,
The one who seeks your heart to gain,
Who year upon year is wholly perverse
In seeking that heart in faltering verse.
Time 'tis to lance this poetic abscess
As faithfulness leads me now to confess:
I am that man, that despicable bard,
That dim-witted, doddering dunce – Richard!
Confessing thus, I'm 'dog in the manger' -
Your true Valentine is no dark stranger,
But rather a bald-headed, blithering prat
Mais qui aime beaucoup sa petite chatte.

Selfish Valentine

Oh! Valentine, can I be thine?
(It makes a change from 'thou be mine')
As I grow older, I decline.
I cling like climbing sweet woodbine.
I promise you I'll toe the line
And everything will turn out fine
If I can be your Valentine.
I pray thee, say 'Be mine! Be mine!'
Since I say truly, 'I am thine.'

Father's Day 2001

A beer
Brings good cheer.
Four
Bring even more.
McEwan's No 1
Is enormous fun
And a Riggwelter
Is a right belter,
While Marston's strong
Lingers long.
An Old Peculiar
Makes me unrulier.
One at a time
Will be sublime.
I couldn't weather
All four together.

Fathers' Day

Bubble, bubble, toil and trouble
If I drink this then I'll see double
Which, when you think the question through,
Is really the best thing to do,
For what's the point of having whisky
If you don't end up feeling frisky?

Thank for my chocolate.
It really is an awful lot
For me to eat, so I'll tell you
My thoughts on what is best to do:
I'll save it till you come again
And share it with my grandchildren.

Father's Day 2004

On Dearest, Darling Daddy's day
I find, this morn, the words to say
How much I like your little card.
You must be finding it quite hard
To find one that is suitable
For one who's proving durable.
As years go by, the variation
Of content makes your situation
Difficult. Could the solution
Be corporeal dissolution?

Forgotten Father
(to the tune of My Bonnie lies over the Ocean)

Oh! You have forgotten your father,
Oh! you've let him go down the nick!
I would have preferred a card rather
Than be cut like this to the quick!
Be cut, be cut, be cut like this to the quick, the quick;
Be cut, be cut, be cut like this to the quick!

Your Grandpa got a card from us two,
He got it right on Father's Day.
I didn't get one and I'm right blue -
Forgotten and far, far away!
'Gotten, 'gotten, 'gotten and far, far away, away;
'Gotten, 'gotten, 'gotten and far, far away!

Why is it that I'm not more adored?
Why does this thought go through my mind:
That I am the one to be ignored?
'Tis really so very unkind!
Really, really, really so very unkind, unkind;
Really, really, really so very unkind!

Hallowe'en 2002

If you come at or after eight
Then I'm afraid you'll be too late
'Cos I'll be watching football.
If after that hour I should hear
The bell then I'm afraid, my dear,
That you'll end up with nowt at all!

Hallowe'en 2003

I

If you are after something nice
Then you are in for a surprise.
If you like slugs, snails, slime and goo,
Then I have just the things for you!
If you want sweeties, come not near
For I don't like things like that here.
All things nasty, all things rotten,
You can be sure that I've got 'em.
And I'm a Scotsman, so, my honeys,
Rest assured you'll get no monies.

II

Hallowe'en is for the youngsters -
Just up to twelve-year-old funsters.
Teenagers now should stay away -
In the past years they've had their day.

III

Really, I must say that I
Cannot quite see eye to eye
With those who, year long, daily preach
That children must avoid the reach
Of evil people, all those who
Seek to attract our youngsters through
Weasel words on screens, or sweets
Offered as they prowl the streets.
They say, 'Don't take sweets from strangers,'
But fail to see th' inherent dangers.
They seem blind and have not seen
The looming threats of Hallowe'en.
They let their children out at night
Roaming streets far out of sight,
Saying to those they choose to meet,
'Come on, mister – trick or treat!'
How do they know that I am
Not that nasty, dirty old man?

Hallowe'en – yet again!

'Tis Hallowe'en
Red, black and green
The ghastly sheen
Of those who've been
But are no more.
Their voices keen
Their wailings mean
They are, I ween,
But ghosts – no more
Now knocking on my door.

Guy Fawkes Night

Please to remember the 5th of November,
You youngsters coming to beg.
I think you should know
That I am very slow!
'Tis the fault of my gammy leg.
So may I implore
Please *don't* BANG on the door.

Carollers' Rhymes

I

Carollers come but once a year
And, when they do, they bring good cheer.
If for their songs reward they seek
Then they must come in Christmas week.
So there's a date you must remember -
Come NOT BEFORE 18TH DECEMBER!

II

'We all want some figgy pudding, so bring some out here!'
For all those who sing that, let me be quite clear:
I am so fed up of hearing that song
Sung year after year and for far too long!
I'll give you a list from which you may choose
And, if you sing one, then you will not lose.
Just one small condition - (I am perverse) -
You must, between you, sing a complete verse!

III

I'll not be stern
And make you learn
Carols you do not know;
But I'll insist
That you persist
Until to me you show
You're not averse
To mast'ring a verse
Of carols shown below!

Yuletide Homilies

I

Spend it well, spend it wisely
Even be a little miserly.
Put a little bit away
To spend it on a later day.

II

Some for today,
Some for tomorrow.
Leave some to pay -
No need to borrow.

III

Don't spend all your money on sweets.
Save some for some other treats.

IV

Don't pontificate to me.
I'm old enough, can't you see,
To spend it as I see fit -
Not as told by an old twit?

11

~ O'er a' the ills o' Life ~

*Kings may be blest, but Tam was glorious
O'er a' the ills o' life victorious!*

Robert Burns

Hypochondria is the one disease I haven't got.

David Renwick

~ *O'er a' the ills o' Life* ~

Healthy Eating

C is for salad – it's what I put in:
Coleslaw, and Carrots, Cucumber sliced thin,
Cress and Cos lettuce and Capsicums raw -
Cum'lative Chlorophyll and so much more.
Cherry tomatoes and Chervil and Chives -
Eat all together to lengthen our lives.
Eschew greasy chips and fat chops' allure
So that man's life-span can longer endure.
Eat salad by day and salad by night.
Whene'er you indulge, it brings pure delight.
So, salad for lunch and salad for tea,
But no Coriander – too strong for me!

Then 'Oy!' came the cry from Sir Celery,
'How is it that you've forgotten me?'
'You're not the only one,' said Cottage Cheese.
'Next time you're at it, remember me, please!'

Dieting

Stomachs growl and husbands howl
As tempers start to fray.
Sod diet! I'll be on the prowl
To make sure Christmas Day
Is one on which the gaze is switched
From frugal fare to cheer.
If there's no hitch at the last ditch,
I'll have my glass of beer!

It's bleedin' obvious

In days long gone
When I was young
My bottom was oozing blood.
It wasn't a trickle
When it started to tickle
But an overwhelming flood.

I went to the doctor and I said, 'Jim,'
(I called him Jim, 'cause I knew him)
'My bottom's bleeding. What's the score?'
He asked me, 'Is it very sore?'
He said, 'Now bend over.' And then he
Stuck a pliable finger in me.

(You what, my dear? Don't worry, love -
He first put on a rubber glove.)

He pushed it right in and turned it about
Totally ignoring my plaintive shout.
With finger removed, he enquired, 'Still sore?'
I replied, ' More sore than it was before!'
He said, ' I know it can hurt like hell,
But you must suffer just to get well.'
I said, 'Am I dying?' With face wreathed in smiles
He replied, reassuring, ' No, just full of piles.'

I relaxed, looked at him and said, 'May I say
It's not a nice way to start your day:
After your breakfast, I show you my arse -
You really can't say, as a start, it's first class.'

He turned to me, smiling, and calmly he said,
'A hole in the bottom differs not from the head.
You must understand it is part of my office.
To examine closely whatever orifice
Comes with a body through my surgery door.
I never complain and, what is more,

I am ever ready to probe and inspect
Whatever folk bring me – what do you expect?
When anyone asks me to look at their ear,
I do so and ensure it's perfectly clear.
And frankly, I must say, goodness only knows
What one can discover stuck up someone's nose!
I've even been asked to plumb a vagina
Seeking a wayward and lost panty-liner!
Your anus, therefore, is no problem - you see,
All holes, top or bottom, are the same to me.'

B* B** B*** Blockage

I felt an urge
A minor surge
But nothing was produced.
I long sat there,
Production rare...
Constipation was adduced.

Mens Lavatoria (First Flush)
(to the tune of My Bonnie lies over the Ocean)

I think that my bowels have lost it,
I think they are well out of line.
I go for my first morning visit
And then I need a second time.
Bring back! Bring back! O bring back
My movements to me, to me;
Bring back! Bring back! O bring back
My movements to me!

Mens Lavatoria (Second Flush)

How nice to hear again the growl
Of a once more active lower bowel!
But every effort made to drain
The lazy colon puts a strain
Upon the anal outer rim,
Which is neither neat nor trim.
For each time Sphincter's wreathed in smiles
It brings another bunch of piles.

P*ssing Thoughts

Lovely jubbly,
Long live Bubbly!
Bubbles
Ease troubles
And make worries flee.
They pass through the kidneys
And so make me pee.
But without urine, where would I be?
Well, no-one could take the piss out of me!

Medical emergency

Dear Dr Hepworth, what can you do?
You told me to keep off the cheese
But I've eaten lots of Blue!
Dear Dr Hepworth, book me for a scan.
Oh, Dr Hepworth, what naughty man I am!

Medical treatment
(to the tune of Sugar in the Morning)

Pop 'em in the morning,
Pop 'em in the evening.
At supper the system prime.
Now the doctor's got me
To make me what I should be,
I'm at it all the time.

Lower your blood pressure,
Get cholesterol's measure,
Rub on the aqueous cream.
Take your pills and potions;
Don't forget the lotions -
Enough to make you scream!

The pills! The pills!

My days are coloured every
One
At break of day and set of
Sun.
The morning sets the day off
Red.
It's white as I go to my
Bed.
Red, white, red white – another
Day
Dies as I make my way towards
Death,
Dies as I go to draw my last
Breath.
But, on the last day, don't be
Blue.
The day I die, I'll still try
To
Prolong my life with the doctor's
Brew.

What did you do on your birthday?
Got up and took a red pill.
Why'd you do that on your birthday?
To stop me from falling ill.
Why'd you feel ill on your birthday?
Because I'm over the hill.
What should you do on your birthday?
Sit down and draw up my will!

Damn the Doctors!

Atenolol
  is taking
    its toll
      of
        my poll.
          The thatch
            is
              no match
                for
                  its clinical
                      snatch.

Lipitor
  is too much
    for
      my mind.
        What remains
          of my brains
            refuses
              to bind.
                I'm left with
                  synapses
                    prone to
                      dire lapses.

Lipitor ad nauseam

Doctors and shareholders rub their hands in glee:
'More money! More divis! - For me and me!'
While I scratch my head in puzzlement
And wonder where my memory went.
The gain is theirs, the loss is mine.
They grow fat and I decline.
I diminish all the time.
Should this go on another year
I'll disappear
'My dear,
I'm here!'

12

~ A most unattractive Old Thing ~

At forty I lost my illusions,
At fifty I lost my hair,
At sixty my hope and teeth were gone
And my feet were beyond repair,
At eighty life has clipped my claws,
I'm bent and bowed and cracked;
But I can't give up the ghost because
My follies are intact.

E. Y. Harburg

H. *We met at nine*
G. *We met at eight*
H. *I was on time*
G. *No, you were late*
H. *Ah yes! I remember it well.*

Alan Jay Lerner

~ A Most Unattractive Old Thing! ~

Life's Little Mysteries

Why is it that hair falls from my head
But then grows from my nose instead?
And, when my pate of thatch is clear
It sprouts like magic from my ear?
My eyebrows are not short of growth
As, Healeyesque,they flourish both.
And certainly there is no lack
Of curling hair upon my back,
While there, across my manly chest
It flourishes, a hirsute vest.
It even decorates my toes!
What good it does there, Heaven knows!
As I grow older, it's not fair
That hair shoots gaily everywhere
Except where it is meant to be -
I'm old, I'm bald. Alas, poor me!

The gift of olfaction

Now that I'm getting old
The gift of Yardley Gold
Makes me think you think
That I absolutely stink.
My sensory decoder
Tells me you perceive odour
The way you pinch your lips thin
Confirms I smell of urine
And your uplifted brows are
Cognizance of soiled trouser;
(Yes, your curled lips' disdain
Notes yellow trouser stain.)
Oh dear! Oh golly gosh!
I promise you I'll wash
And so the smell can't hover
I'll splash it on all over!

Senex

As time goes by, men's bodies fold:
That is the price of growing old.
Their bellies sag, their boobies droop,
Their backsides drop and need a scoop
To keep them in their trousers' grip.
It really does give me the pip
That even when food intake's less
I end up looking such a mess.
The top half's fat, the bottom's thin;
No muscle now round thigh and shin,
The skin-tone's gone, just wrinkles there
Together with a lack of hair.
I can but enter this last plea -
Look on me as I used to be.

Flatulence

As we grow old, 'tis often said
That, as we lie there in our bed,
We should be seeking to achieve
Concordant farts more than, with heave
And with thrust, the fleeting spasm
Of simultaneous orgasm.

Calmer Karma

When I was young and in my prime
It was Karma Sutra all the time.
But now I'm getting old and grey
A calmer sutra suits my day.

Ultima Debilitas

Legs long and lithe and lissom lead
To where one longs to plant one's seed.
But though desire and thoughts are bold,
I find the body growing old.
I fear that now, when I'm in bed
The action takes place in my head.
Alas! As I lie there, I find
That, sadly, it's all in the mind.

Degeneration has stepped in,
What once stood firm hangs limp and thin.
No longer proudly on the prowl,
It cowers now beneath its cowl.
And there, below, the wizened sack
Wreathed in grey hair, is dangling, slack.

My flaccid, floppy phallus is no good.
It cowers now 'neath its preputial hood.
It fails at blood engorgement and won't rise,
Thus robbing me of manly man's great prize.
But there is one duty it will not miss:
It will, I'm sure, go on taking the piss!

Old Bones

Old bones creak
And old bones crack.
Joints grow weak
In an old man's back.
Fingers tremble,
Shoulders hurt.
Quick! Assemble
St John's Wort!

Taking myself in hand

(in response to a newspaper article recommending masturbation as beneficial to prostate health)

I followed the advice to the elderly
To caress myself quite tenderly.
I know not if it improved my prostate
But it left me completely prostrate!

Senesco V

God! I'm old!
I saw a recent photo
And I thought:
That's not me.
I stand up straight,
My eyes are keen,
I look the world straight in the face -
But I don't;
Not any more.

I never thought that you would see
A 'modern' poem writ by me.
But, then again, you never know
What passing years force me to show.

Fading Powers

My propensity
For serendipity
In what concerns rhyme
Diminishes with time.
As days go by
I find I cannot fly
Quite so high as in years gone by.

Here's a health unto the elderly!

In Selby, that enlightened town,
The O.A.P.'s keep their costs down.
Old, but wise and canny are we -
A haircut for three pounds fifty!

Some time ago, as I sat there
Ensconced in comfy barber's chair,
Since all around were aged men
We talked about our regimen.

'When I fell ill and went to see
What medicine could do for me,
I went with what I thought to be
Essential tremor – Ah! Poor me!

'With Doctor this and Doctor that,
All wearing medicine's recent hat,
I came out with high blood pressure -
Cholesterol beyond measure!

Statins for cholesterol,
For blood pressure – Atenolol.'
Atenolol! Their cry rang out.
With might and main, an awesome shout!

Their heads wagged whitely, side by side.
'And me!' 'And me!' the old men cried.
The moral of this tale's soon told:
You're not alone when you grow old.

Gammy Joint

Embolism has taken flight
So my status quo is
I no longer fight
To pull those socks over
My feet. I'm in clover!

The Joys of Old Age

I'm concocting an old person's rhyme:
'Think and do just one thing at a time.'
For, if not, you will stand on the stair
Asking what you are doing up there.

I'm creaking, I'm cramping, I have purple toes.
The longer I live, that is just how it goes!
Fasciculation has set in.
Within my calves, below the skin,
The muscles twist with hill and hollow
Like active worms within their burrow.
My fibres now like music segue
With ceaseless movement in my leg.
Are 'restless legs' now bound to be
A source of misery for me?
It moves around my body, so
It's not confined to down below.
Upon my brow, where old scar lies,
It rolls and ripples o'er my eyes.
Soon, like a snake, I could lie down
And writhe myself from here to town.

Never close your eyes while upright
Or you'll fall flat on your face,
And make sure that you're standing
On a perfectly firm base.
Growing old is not amusing;
If you live, you'll find that true.
If you ignore these instructions,
I'm sure that you'll certainly rue
Your totally bland assumption
That you know better than this
And consider advice given
As merely taking the piss!

Don't stand up too quickly – you'll leave your head behind.
You'll find folk are friendly, and very, very kind.
They'll pick you up, dust you down and say, 'Never mind!'
But, for all their kindness, it's still an awful bind!

Once Up-on...

Time was, when on awaking,
I'd slip eel-like from my bed.
Now, like an upturned tortoise,
I so feebly flail instead.
Before, my legs obeyed me;
Now I stagger as I go
Weaving slowly round the bedroom
Till the blood begins to flow.

That's life!

It creeps upon you unawares.
The years pass by and never count.
'Oh, you're so young,' they say.
But, as time passes
Still replaces *so*
And thus, unheeding, you then go
Into the next stage of your life,
Unconscious of the years' accumulation.
'No,' they say, 'you are not old.'
But there, at last, the dread word comes.
And then your old friend *so* comes back:
'You're not *so* old!'
So young – *so* old -
Where are the years that passed between?
But passed they are
And in their place come ills and pain.
You fight against them and, in return,
The kind remarks abound:
'I never thought you were that age!'
'You do very well, dear, for your age.'
'What do you expect then, at your age?'
So there it is at last;
The sly serpent of your life
Takes centre stage and dominates.
Now that he has come, little remains
But death.

Hair today, Gone tomorrow

Atenolol
Has taken its toll
Of my residual hair.
Swallowed each day,
There's a price to pay,
Now there's almost nothing there.
But yet this is true
And is something I rue
For really it's not quite fair
Since, when comes the call
For my visit to Paul,
It's still full price to cut hair!

Apologia

How unkind, for it's not true -
Those are words which I shall rue.
The Paul I know is much kinder;
A mirror gives me a reminder
My hair is cut with art and skill
So, when I look, it seems I've still
The odd few locks to grace my head
(They'll last me until I am dead!)
So I'll say naught but 'Thankyou, Paul,
I'll see you next when hair must fall.'

As time goes by

The older you get
The more you forget
And all other folk
Don't believe you.
It's not your fault, mate,
That the Time – clock shows 'late'
And memories show up so few.

Bloody Background Music!

My dear BBC,
Why is it that we
Should have to suffer
The awful buffer
Of music next
To spoken text?
The background played
Simply puts paid
To efforts to hear
The words, I fear.

Listen up!

'Oh! Look!' I said. 'A parcel!
Is it something for me?'
'Ear, ear,' she mouthed. I replied,
'There's no need to agree!
I want to know what's in there.'
She mimed again, 'Ear, ear.'
I said, 'That's no good to me!'
Loud, she said. 'You will see!'
I followed her instructions -
'Twas earphones for deaf me!
I wear them all the time now,
They dangle from my ears.
They do the job they're meant to :
They beat the passing years.
The only trouble now is
That, as I watch the screen,
I've to take them off again
To discuss what I've seen!

Deafness

Deafness is just like a silken cloud
That settles on you so gently.
As time goes by, it thickens more,
Layer upon layer it lies
Until the dreaded time arrives
When *Pardon?* Is your most used word.
Pardon you seek, pardon you get
Until the strain becomes too much...
And then you find yourself alone
In a new world.

Always look on the bright side

Lipitor led to great memory loss,
But also brought some advantages:
I now find I can take my books
Sit down and then turn the pages -

       The text is all new
           and totally due
               to my amnesia
                     seizure.

And that, in its turn
Gives me money to burn.
But oh! All those writers
Reduced now to hovels
Since, these days, poor blighters,
I don't buy their novels!

Sinister Urination – a Mystery Solved?

What can explain it? Ah! Now I see -
Seventy-four years of having a pee.
Right-handed shaking – it has so affected
The angle at which the flow is directed.
Had I been left-handed, the chances are bright
The flow would then go, not to left, but to right.
The only thing missing is enough time left
For putting my theory to a stringent test.
Seventy-four years represent but a half;
One – four – eight and testing? You've just got laugh!
I've had an idea! It really is great!
I'll use both my hands, and then I'll pee straight!

Mens Lavatoria

Oh! it's not what I'd call bog-paper first class
When your fingers go through it and straight up your arse.
Good paper is strong and can resist pressure
And so you can wipe your arse at your leisure
Without the threat of a shit-stained fore-finger
And noxious aromas that do tend to linger.

New town?
(or incipient Alzheimer's?)

Why when visiting (for you) a new town,
Turn up at a corner instead of turn down?
Why cross the street to go and stare
When really there's naught of interest there?
Then, having walked a goodly mile,
Your wife turns towards you with a loving smile
And says, 'You forget , we've been here.
We both saw it all, at the same time last year.'

Septuagenarian

I have now joined the happy clan
Of those who've reached th' allotted span
But know not if I can handle
The dictum of game and candle.
'Gainst creaking joints and cramp and pain
I have to weigh whether I gain
From going on and struggling through
The years ahead – but then, there's you.
With you beside me, I can bear
Whatever fate awaits out there.

It's the Alzheimer's

As I grow old it's quite absurd
How I forget the correct - er?

And again, on forgetting a grandchild's birthday:

Grandpaternally
I'm infernally
Late.

I should be hissed
For having missed
The date.

To try and mend
My gaffe, I send
This cheque.

A small amount
For their account -
By 'eck!

Peter 2004

O rage! O desespoir!
These words have the power
To encapsulate
My brother's mental state.

The thing that hurts – he looks the same
And yet, when I pronounce my name,
He looks at me with dull eyes blue
'Neath lowered lids, while striving to
Harness the thoughts and to express
The fleeting wisps of consciousness.
Then, can there be words sadder than,
'I...do...not - do...not...know...that...man'?

Intimations of Alzheimer's

Remember me as I have been
Not what I may become.
For what is good is what is done -
The past is ever green.

13

~ *I told you!* ~

BLUEBOTTLE: *You rotten swines. I told you I'd be deaded.*

Spike Milligan

Death has got something to be said for it:
There's no need to get out of bed for it;
Wherever you may be,
They bring it to you, free.

Kingsley Amis

When the fat lady sings

I would wish my body laid
In a green-leaved country glade,
In some field devoted to
All like-minded people who,
At the end of their life's span,
Prefer that place, rather than
A grave beneath a tombstone hard
In some neat, straight-lined churchyard.
In a box of paper made
With no mark of pomp displayed,
That my fading flesh may feed
Worms and grass and flow'ring seed
Till, at last, my spirit, free,
Blooms above in flower and tree.

Death wish

I shall leave with little comment passed
upon me when I've gone.
There'll remain but slender traces of the
work that I have done.
Does the lack of renown matter? No, it
certainly does not.
What the people think about me matters
not a single jot.
There's but one thing I would ask for as the
end comes to my life:
Let it be, oh! I beseech you, that I
die before my wife.
She, without me, would fare very well.
I, without her, would be living in Hell.

Epitaph

Bury me upright so that I may take
Only the space I used when I walked straight.
Let my body be blessed at the Church.
Let my grave-fellow be a silver birch.
So will the years that it grows, till it's death,
Match the years spent till I drew my last breath.

Mors Venit

What a fine day
(Won't it be fun!)
When the great day has come
And I've passed away.
Those who survive
(Glad to be still alive)
Gather to make hay.
What they do not know,
Assembled for the show,
Is what's in the Will!
What is there today?
Their greedy hands clutch
At what is not much.
'Not much!' Must I say,
'It has all gone astray -
I've used it to pay
My wife's and my way!'

Aftermath

When I am dead, think only this of me:
That all things left behind don't need to be
Stored, hoarded, treasured in my memory.
I would like to see all burned or broken
Rather than that memories be woken
By these things gathered as a token
Of my past life.

It doesn't matter

It doesn't matter when you're born and still less when you die
If, in between you can enjoy the sun, the sea, the sky
And all the wonders of the world and of the universe
before, at last, your time is come, and you're put in the hearse.

It's obvious

Some die soon and
Some die late.
Some in love and
Some in hate.
Some in peace and
Some in pain.
But
All end up dead
Just the same!

14

~ Count the Ways ~

How do I love thee? Let me count the ways.

Elizabeth Barrett Browning

*But to see her was to love her,
Love but her, and love for ever.*

Robert Burns

~ Count the ways ~

A cautionary tale

In days gone by his hair was blond
Which explains why his wife was fond
Of patting him upon the head
Before she hauled him off to bed.

What happened's not for me to show
And surely not for you to know,
But patting it wore out his hair
And now there is no blond thatch there.

So now no longer is he led
By his fond wife up to her bed.
The moral of this tale is clear:
Just leave my hair alone, my dear!

Blue Room

Blue room -
I saw it all in my mind.
I never thought I would find
My blue room quite so soon.

Before you came, it was all quite chaotic.
Then you were there like some wondrous new broom
Just as I was becoming psychotic.
Before my eyes you created Blue Room.

Blue room -
I saw it all in my mind.
I never thought I would find
My blue room quite so soon.

The difference between us

Whatever *I* save is rubbish
And really must be thrown away.
Whatever *she* saves is vital
To be kept for another day.

My Mrs Atkinson

I love you, Mrs Atkinson,
And more and more each day.
There's nothing you could do to me
That would drive me away.
Ending mutual life cannot be contemplated,
Hard luck, my dear, to live with me you are fated!

One of these days

One of these days I'm going to be right
But until now it has never been true.
Though I'll try all day and I'll try all night,
My wife will say, 'I know better than you.'

Night time

To wake at night and find you there,
To feel the caress of your hair,
To feel your hand within my own
Can, between us, only hone
My love for you.

Time goes by

I'm sorry that we now no more
Join as one as we did before,
But your presence by my side
Tells me that you still abide
By what we felt those years gone by
That I shall feel until I die.
So your hand seeks out my own
Proving that we now have grown
From our two bodies to but one -
So to perfection we have come.

My wife – My life

If ever I say 'Darling! I now wish to die',
Please do not think that it's addressed to all but my
Wish to take from you the burden of our state
Since you know what you're doing
And I'm forever late
At knowing what there is to do
And what must needs be done.
I can but find the name that's you
As she who stands alone.

When I am dead

When I am dead, my darling,
Think only this, and see
That I bored you far, far more
Than ever you bored me.

Where is she?

Where is the girl
that I first met late one autumn long ago?
Where is the girl
who smiled at me from her seat *au Grand Cafe?*
Where is the girl
whose letters lie with mine within a secret box?
Where is the girl
who long time lay within my arms contentedly?
Where is the girl
who gave to me my children and who cared for them?
Where is the girl
whose smile forgave me when my manly strength had fled?
Where is the girl
who shared with me the joys and sorrows of my working life?
Where is the girl
whose works surround me and give pleasure to my eyes?

She sits beside me – and I know just how much I owe to her.

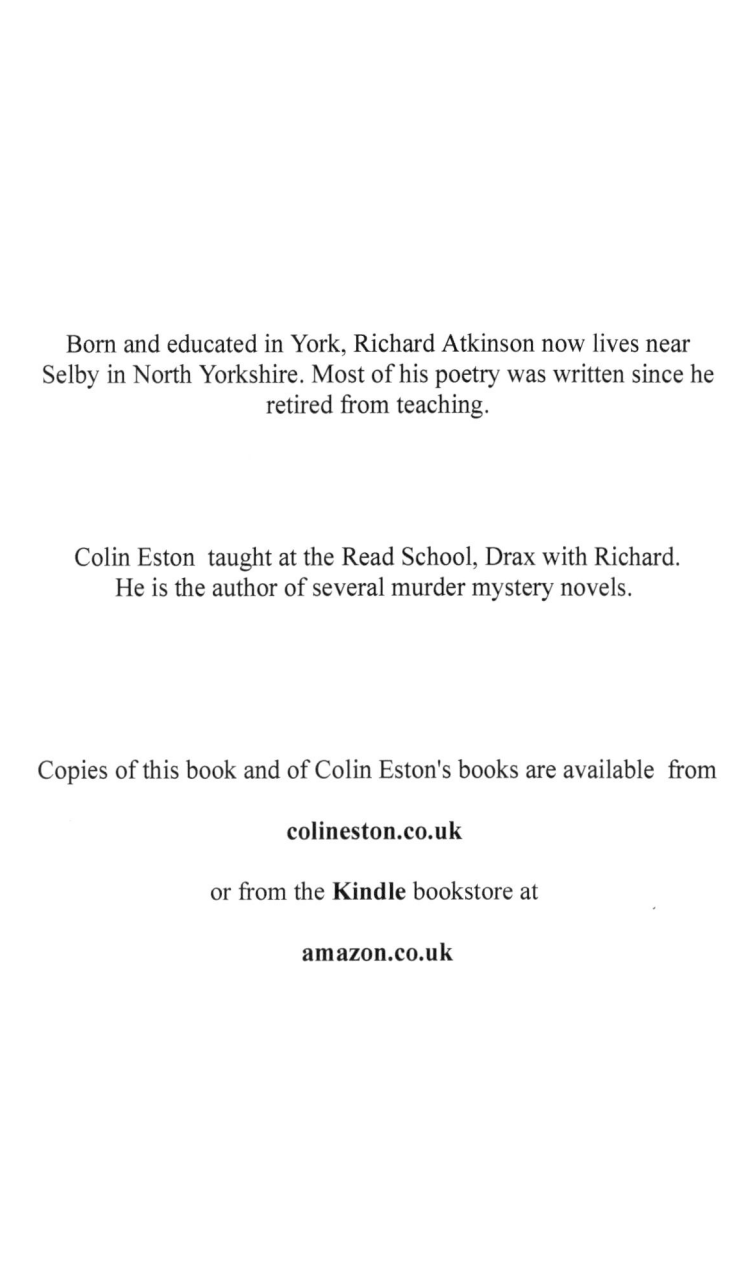

Born and educated in York, Richard Atkinson now lives near Selby in North Yorkshire. Most of his poetry was written since he retired from teaching.

Colin Eston taught at the Read School, Drax with Richard. He is the author of several murder mystery novels.

Copies of this book and of Colin Eston's books are available from

colineston.co.uk

or from the **Kindle** bookstore at

amazon.co.uk

Made in the USA
Charleston, SC
14 August 2012